I Am Worthy

365 DAYS OF SELF-CARE AFFIRMATIONS FOR EMPOWERED WOMEN

Uplifting Your True Self:
Discover the Power of Self-Love,
Confidence, and Resilience

EMMA BENNETT

CHAPTER ZERO

Copyright © 2023 by Chapter Zero

All rights reserved. No part of this publication may be reproduced, distributed, or transmitted in any form or by any means, including photocopying, recording, or other electronic or mechanical methods, without the prior written permission of the publisher, except in the case of brief quotations embodied in critical reviews and certain other noncommercial uses permitted by copyright law. For permission requests, write to the publisher at the address below.

Chapter Zero LLC
16192 Coastal Highway
Lewes, 19958
Delaware – USA
Contact: info@chapterzerobooks.com

Paperback ISBN 978-1-961963030
Hardcover ISBN 978-1-961963047

Contents

Introduction	1
1. The Science And Soul Of Affirmations	5
The Science Behind Affirmations	
Guidelines for Self-Care and Transformation	
2. Unveiling Self-Worth And Confidence	15
Affirmations	
3. Embracing Body Positivity And Self-Acceptance	27
Affirmations	
4. Grounding In Mindfulness And Presence	39
Affirmations	
5. Harnessing Resilience In Overcoming Challenges	51
Affirmations	

6. Nurturing Relationships And Setting Boundaries Affirmations ... 63

7. Thriving In Career And Personal Ambitions Affirmations ... 75

8. Prioritizing Self In Daily Life Affirmations ... 87

9. Discovering Purpose And Inner Peace Affirmations ... 99

Conclusion ... 111

Bonus - Nine Transformative Routines for Women ... 113

Introduction

Hello, beautiful souls. My name is Emma, and I am honored to be your guide on this transformative journey of self-care, self-love, and self-awareness. Like many of you, I've walked the path of self-doubt, struggled with societal expectations, and grappled with the overwhelming pressures of modern life. But through it all, I discovered the power of affirmations and their profound impact on our psyche, confidence, and daily lives.

My journey toward self-love and self-awareness wasn't a straight path. It was filled with twists and turns, highs and lows, moments of clarity, and days of confusion. But every step, every challenge, and every tear shed was a lesson that brought me closer to understanding my true self. And it's this journey, with all its imperfections and revelations, that I wish to share with you through this book.

Affirmations, simple as they may seem, have been my anchor during turbulent times. I recall a particularly challenging period in my life when everything seemed to be falling apart. My self-esteem was at an all-time low, and the weight of societal expectations felt suffocating. One evening, as I sat by my window, a gentle whisper of a thought emerged: "I am enough." This simple affirmation became my mantra. Every morning, I would repeat it to myself, and with each repetition, its power grew. Over time, this affirmation transformed my mindset, my actions, and my interactions with the world around me. It was a turning point that highlighted the profound impact of positive self-talk.

This book is a culmination of my experiences, insights, and the powerful affirmations that have been instrumental in my personal growth journey. Each section is meticulously crafted to address the unique challenges and aspirations of "Empowered Emma" and every woman who sees a reflection of herself in my story.

Within these pages, you'll find affirmations to lift your confidence, foster body positivity, ground you in mindfulness, strengthen your resilience, nurture relationships, support your ambitions, prioritize self-care, and so much more. Each day offers a new opportunity to unveil your magnificence.

I invite you to begin this transformative journey with an open heart and an open mind. Let these affirmations be your guiding light, illuminating the path to self-love, confidence, and resilience. Remember, the power to uplift, inspire, and celebrate your true self lies within you. All you need to do is unveil it.

So take a deep breath, and let's begin the beautiful process of unveiling the best version of you. Together, we'll get through this one day - and one affirmation - at a time.

Chapter One

The Science And Soul Of Affirmations

For much of history, society viewed self-care as an extravagance - the domain of the wealthy who could afford things like lavish vacations, spa treatments, or shopping sprees. Taking time for oneself was seen as selfish or frivolous.

But our understanding of health and wellbeing has expanded over the past few decades. We now recognize that regularly attending to our mental, emotional, and physical needs is not a luxury but a necessity.

Far from being pampering or indulgent, true self-care is about keeping our most basic needs met. It can be as simple as getting enough sleep, taking deep breaths when stressed, setting healthy boundaries, or expressing gratitude for the good in our lives.

Science confirms that small daily self-care practices strengthen our resilience to life's challenges. Skipping out on self-care leaves us depleted and puts our health at risk over the long term.

So let's banish any lingering guilt or belief that self-care is just for the privileged. Honor what your mind and body need to function and thrive. You deserve to care for yourself with the same compassion you would extend to a loved one.

Make self-care a daily non-negotiable. Your inner light can only shine when your whole self is nourished. Together, we can unveil our best selves through simple, consistent practices.

The Science Behind Affirmations

Affirmations have long been used as tools for positive change, but recent research is shedding new light on why and how these simple practices can be so transformative.

Science tells us our repetitive thoughts and beliefs shape our brains. When we repeatedly tell ourselves something is true - even if it's not - our brains will eventually start to accept it as reality. Affirmations work by harnessing this phenomenon, gradually dismantling negative thought patterns and replacing them with more empowering beliefs.

Studies show that with consistent practice, affirmations rewire neural pathways, altering ingrained modes of thinking and behavior. New connections are formed every time you consciously choose an uplifting thought over a limiting one.

Affirmations are especially powerful when focused inward. Positive self-talk activates regions of the brain linked to higher self-esteem, motivation, and emotional resilience. Telling yourself "I am worthy" or "I am empowered" stimulates the reward centers in your brain, boosting feelings of joy and self-acceptance.

Of course, adopting more positive beliefs requires effort and consistency. Our default reaction is often to resist change or new ways of thinking. The key is repetition. When you start each day by reading a positive affirmation, you plant the seeds for transformation.

Over time, those seeds blossom into more uplifted moods, positive behaviors, and greater life satisfaction. Research shows that people who practice regular affirmations report boosts in confidence, body image, and ability to manage stress.

The science and data speak for themselves - with a commitment to daily affirmations, you can rewrite old stories of self-doubt and unlock your highest potential. This book provides the tools; your dedication will fuel positive changes.

While the introspective work begins with you, the possibilities are endless. Spreading more light and empowerment starts by unveiling your own inner radiance. Are you ready to lead yourself to greater joy, purpose, and potential? This transformative journey begins now.

Guidelines for Self-Care and Transformation

This book provides 365 affirmations to unlock your highest potential and unveil your inner magnificence. To fully embrace this transformative journey, here are some recommendations:

Set a Consistent Routine

Carve out 5-10 quiet minutes every morning to read and absorb that day's affirmation. Find a peaceful space to go undisturbed and genuinely focus on yourself. Silence your phone, set your intention, and clear your mind before beginning. Treat this ritual as non-negotiable self-care to start your day centered and grounded. Over time, it will become second nature.

Read Slowly with Presence

When reading the daily affirmation, don't just rush through the words. Give each sentence thoughtful attention. Read the affirmation aloud, even if just whispering to yourself. Let the meaning behind each phrase fully register. Allow yourself to feel the emotional resonance of the words. Pause and take a breath between sentences to let the affirmation penetrate deeply. Silently repeat impactful words or lines. Savor the affirmation by reading it multiple times if it really strikes a chord. The goal is mindful, meditative absorption of the empowering message.

Journal for Clarity

Writing down affirmations and reflections can help further imprint the messages in your mind. Keep a dedicated journal just for this practice. Each day, copy down the affirmation word-for-word into your journal before reading it aloud. After reading it, jot down any thoughts, feelings, or intentions that arise. As you move through the year, your journal will become a tangible record of your growth and inner unveiling journey. Periodically read back through past entries to see how far you've come and prepare yourself for the next phase. Let the journal be a wellspring of inspiration you can turn to any time your commitment wavers.

Repeat Throughout Your Day

Don't let your affirmation practice end when your morning ritual does. Return to the affirmation throughout your day, repeating it silently or aloud whenever you need a boost of empowerment. Calling the affirmation to mind can help center and ground you when challenges arise. When self-doubt creeps in, reciting the affirmation will keep you on track. When you need motivation, inspiration, or an uplifting reminder of your worth, your affirmation will be there, ready to lift you up. Let it be your anchor in turbulent seas and your guiding light when the path forward seems hazy. By integrating the affirmations into your daily life, their positive effects will gradually spill over into all areas.

Visualize the Possibilities

Affirmations plant seeds that can blossom into tangible change over time. To accelerate the process, take some time to vividly visualize your future self living each affirmation. Close your eyes, take some deep breaths, and imagine scenarios where your new beliefs and empowered mindset are fully embodied. See yourself radiating self-confidence, setting boundaries, speaking your needs, and leading your desired life. Make the visualizations as detailed as possible - notice the expressions on people's faces, sounds, colors, and textures. The brain has trouble differentiating between vivid visualization and actual experience, so this mental imagery strengthens neural pathways to make your vision a reality.

Stay Patient With Yourself

Change won't happen overnight. Years of conditioned thinking can't be rewritten in a day. This journey will have ups and downs, so you must meet setbacks and struggles with compassion. Don't get discouraged if you slip into old thought patterns or have days of ineffective affirmations. Expect this, and be kind to yourself. Each moment you choose positivity over negativity is progress. When you need motivation, reflect on how far you've already come. Trust that important inner shifts are unfolding even if the outer change isn't evident yet. Know that you're strong enough to stay consistent. With loving patience and commitment to the practice, your growth is inevitable.

Adapt Affirmations To Resonate

The affirmations in this book are meant to inspire and empower but feel free to adapt them to resonate even more deeply with your unique needs and personality. Change pronouns, tweak sentence structure, replace words - do whatever helps the affirmations land powerfully for you. You might identify certain themes you want to expand on or language that motivates you more. For example, if nature metaphors speak to you, work those in. The key is finding phrasing that aligns with your spirit. While staying true to the affirmations' positive essence, mold them into messages that feel like they were written just for you. Soon they will effortlessly lift you up.

Ritualize for Motivation

To maintain inspiration and celebrate your growth, develop special monthly or seasonal rituals that reflect on progress made and focus energy on the path ahead. For example, each new moon perform a releasing ceremony - write down limiting beliefs on paper, then burn or bury the paper under the moonlight. Or at each equinox or solstice, create an altar with meaningful objects, meditate by candlelight, and visualize the next phase of your journey. Develop rituals that feel nurturing and empowering. Activities like bathing by candlelight, meditating, dancing, creating art, or spending quality time with loved ones can help you feel present and prepared for positive change. Rituals energize your spirit and remind you of how far you've come.

Believe In Your Worth

Never forget that you deserve inner peace, contentment, and abundant joy right now, just as you are. All the light you seek is already within you, ready to be unveiled. Even if society tries to attach your worth to certain achievements, know that you are complete and worthy beyond measure. When self-doubt creeps in, consciously choose to believe in your inherent magnificence. Remind yourself that setbacks are temporary, but your inner light is eternal. Trust that you have the strength and wisdom to navigate this journey. You are worthy, capable, and so very loved - keep these truths close to your heart when the path gets difficult. Your courageous commitment speaks to your splendor.

MY NOTES

Self-care
IS EMPOWERMENT

Chapter Two

Unveiling Self-Worth And Confidence

As women, we are conditioned by society to minimize our strengths, downplay our achievements, and question our inherent worth. Negative self-talk often becomes ingrained, eroding our confidence. But the truth is - you are so much more radiant and capable than your inner critic gives you credit for.

This chapter provides empowering affirmations to help silence that skeptical voice and unveil your purposeful, valuable self. By combating feelings of inadequacy, you can stop dwelling on perceived flaws and start appreciating your unique gifts.

Rather than harshly judging yourself, learn to acknowledge your accomplishments, no matter how small. Celebrate the special qualities that make you who you are. Recognize that you add meaning and joy to the world simply by being your authentic self.

The coming affirmations aim to dismantle any notion that you are not good enough. Feelings of self-doubt and insecurity do not define you. Daily practice will give you a deep knowledge of your inherent worth and brilliance.

You contain limitless potential. As you commit to celebrating your strengths, you take steps to boldly pursue your dreams unencumbered. This journey is about unveiling the unstoppable force of nature that you are. Together, let's cultivate radical self-love and unshakeable confidence in your power. The only voice that matters is the one telling you that you are ENOUGH. Are you ready to tune into that voice and finally believe it?

Affirmations

I release all self-judgment and choose to embrace my inner light.

My confidence grows from within as I acknowledge my innate worth.

I celebrate all that makes me uniquely and authentically me.

My inner critic no longer holds power over me. I am enough.

I boldly take up space in this world, knowing I belong and matter.

My strengths far outweigh my weaknesses. I focus on my gifts.

Each day I express my voice, values, and vision. My contributions are valid.

I release concern for others' approval. My belief in myself is all I need.

My power comes from speaking my truth, not from pleasing others.

I embrace myself fully, imperfections and all. I am a work of art.

I acknowledge my past mistakes with grace, knowing they have strengthened me.

My confidence grows as I courageously face life's challenges.

I celebrate my accomplishments, no matter how small. Each step forward matters.

I acknowledge my progress and remember how far I've come.

I trust in my intuition. My inner wisdom always guides me toward truth.

I lean into my fears and follow my heart anyway. Courage is my superpower.

Every day I recognize my capabilities. I achieve what I believe I can.

I welcome abundance into my life knowing I'm worthy of prosperity.

My positive self-talk drowns out any inner criticism. I choose to believe in myself.

I forgive the times I've doubted myself. My past does not determine my future.

I release the need to be perfect. Progress over perfection is my new mantra.

I embrace uncertainty, knowing I have the resilience to handle whatever comes my way.

I give myself full permission to take up space and shine brightly.

My confidence is not dependent on others. I am whole and complete in myself.

I celebrate this journey of self-discovery. Each step forward unveils my magnificence.

I acknowledge my own significance. My life has purpose and meaning.

I welcome an abundance of loving, supportive relationships into my life.

My needs are valid. I honor myself by setting boundaries and asking for support.

I release the idea that I must earn self-worth. I embrace my wholeness.

I trust in my capability to achieve my goals and dreams. My power comes from within.

I forgive and free myself from past hurts. I will not let others' actions define me.

I embrace constructive criticism while filtering out destructive judgments. I know myself.

I give myself full permission to rest and recharge. My health comes before hustle.

I acknowledge my own resilience. Time and again, I've persisted through life's challenges.

I celebrate other women's accomplishments while taking pride in my own. There is plenty of success to go around.

I welcome healthy competition knowing my worth is never on the line. Win or lose, I'm enough.

I release the need to grasp for control. I trust in life's unfolding and my adaptability.

I surround myself with supportive souls who celebrate the real me.

I let go of relationships that require me to shrink. Authentic connections enrich my spirit.

I acknowledge my interdependence with others. Alone, I am enough. Together, we are bountiful.

I embrace that there will always be more growth ahead. The journey of self-discovery never ends.

Uncertainty about the future no longer unsettles me. I flow with life's changes.

Each day I recognize my progress. Little by little, I'm stepping into my power.

I celebrate others without harboring jealousy. There is plenty of joy and success for all.

Perfectionistic thinking no longer holds me back. Progress, not perfection, is the goal.

With compassion for myself and others, I boldly speak my truth.

I embrace all aspects of my identity. I am beautifully and wonderfully made.

MY NOTES

Self-care
IS EMPOWERMENT

Chapter Three

Embracing Body Positivity And Self-Acceptance

Far too often, society's narrow definitions of beauty lead us to fixate on perceived physical flaws rather than appreciate the incredible capabilities of our bodies. We are bombarded with images that make us feel the need to change ourselves just to live up to some unrealistic ideal.

But your sense of self-worth was never meant to depend on your appearance. This chapter provides empowering affirmations to help you challenge those restrictive social standards and celebrate your body for all it allows you to experience and accomplish.

The coming affirmations will guide you in releasing judgment about your looks and fostering gratitude for your body's health, strength, and vitality. You can learn to nurture your physical, mental, and emotional wellbeing as you let go of unhelpful comparisons and perfectionistic thinking.

This journey is about remembering that true beauty radiates from within. It's time to stop fixating on supposed flaws and start appreciating your body as the magnificent vessel it is. You deserve to feel at home and at ease in your skin. Are you ready to embrace body positivity and unconditional self-acceptance? Your unique beauty is waiting to be unveiled.

Affirmations

I release unrealistic expectations about my body. As is, I am perfectly whole.

I celebrate my body's strength, health, and life force.

I choose to shift my inner dialogue from criticism to gratitude for this miracle of a body.

I honor my body's needs for nourishment, movement, rest, and care.

I appreciate all my body allows me to experience in this world. Each sensation is a gift.

I free myself from the need to live up to society's definitions of attractive. I embrace my unique beauty.

My sense of self-worth stems from who I am, not how I look.

I release concern over my weight, measurements, or any other numbers. My body is so much more than data.

I make peace with the parts of me that used to make me uncomfortable. I am worthy as is.

I trust my body's innate wisdom. Every message and sensation provides meaningful guidance.

I nurture body, mind and spirit. My care and compassion extend to all facets of my being.

I forgive my body and free it from the burden of past judgments. A clean slate begins now.

I exercise for health, strength and joy - never to punish my body or shrink its shape.

I nourish my body with foods that uplift and energize me. Fuel for radiant wellbeing.

I embrace my natural rhythms of rest, activity, and renewal. Honoring my body's cycles.

I compare myself only to my past self, appreciating my progress and growth.

My body is a vehicle for achievement, self-care, and bringing more light into the world.

I embrace my body's perfect imperfection. Flaws are what make me beautifully human.

I take pride in my body's power. My physical capabilities are something to celebrate.

I release worry over aspects of my appearance I cannot control. Self-acceptance is the path to peace.

I surround myself with media and messages that reflect the diversity and beauty of all bodies.

I lift up other women in their body-positivity journeys, knowing empowerment is not limited.

I wear clothes that make me feel joyful, at ease and express my spirit.

I move my body to feel alive and free, not to manipulate my shape. The joy is in the experience.

I lovingly care for this temporary body so my spirit can thrive during our time together in this world.

I unveil my body's unique magnificence with tenderness and acceptance. Our differences are cause for celebration.

I acknowledge my body's purpose is far greater than appearance. It enables me to live, learn, love.

With gratitude, I marvel at my body's resilience through illness, injury, and all of life's trials.

I release judgment about my age. Every season of life brings new possibilities for growth.

I patiently reprogram my thoughts when old body criticisms creep back in. This too shall pass.

I honor my changing, aging body with the same love I give my youthful one.

I let go of unrealistic standards around my sexuality, sensuality, and reproduction. My body's worth, and purpose remain whole.

I forgive my body and free it from guilt for any past actions. We walk forward in harmony.

My appearance does not dictate my capabilities or character. The beauty of spirit matters most.

I release needless comparisons to other women. We each walk our own path in this temporary body.

I fearlessly embrace styles, grooming, and self-care that align with my spirit. My body celebrates my individuality.

With compassion, I nurture a positive relationship with food based on balance and moderation.

I honor my body's need for rest. Rest is productive when it fuels my wellbeing.

I unconditionally accept the current shape and size of my body. As my needs change, so may my body.

I override inherited and societal body expectations by focusing on how I feel, not how I look.

My body teaches me to live fully in each moment, not put off joy waiting for a different form.

I mindfully listen to my body's signals. Intuition guides me better than external pressures.

Health indicators beyond my weight, like energy, strength and sleep, now shape my self-care.

I embrace my sexuality as I become more intimate with my wants, needs, comforts and boundaries.

Each day, I recognize this wondrous body I inhabit. Awe and appreciation fill my heart.

With loving words and actions, I cultivate self-acceptance and unconditional reverence for my body's sanctity.

MY NOTES

Self-care
IS EMPOWERMENT

Chapter Four

Grounding In Mindfulness And Presence

Our busy modern lives often leave us scattered, stressed, and disconnected from the present moment. We get caught up in lengthy to-do lists, digital distractions, and worries about the future. Before we know it, days or weeks can pass without us ever feeling fully grounded or mindful.

But there is beauty to be unveiled in nearly every moment if we learn to pause and tune into it. This chapter provides affirmations to help reduce overwhelming feelings and ground you firmly in the richness of the here and now.

The coming affirmations will guide you in taking purposeful breaks, quieting your racing mind, and opening your senses to the splendor around you. As you let go of constant busyness and future tripping, you create space to appreciate subtle daily joys and blessings.

Let's remember that life comprises individual moments, each offering an opportunity. It's time to stop rushing past the present in hopes for some distant "when." Your task is to fully inhabit each moment and unwrap the gifts waiting for you there. Are you ready to awaken to the beauty within and around you? The power of now awaits.

Affirmations

I take purposeful breaks to quiet my mind and come into the present.

I let go of busyness and future worries, focusing my energy on the here and now.

I open my senses and take in the splendid details all around me.

I pause to appreciate the sun on my skin, the breeze through my hair, and all of nature's beauty.

I embrace moments of stillness and solitude, where I can connect deeply with myself.

I tune into my breath, using it to center myself in challenging moments.

I channel racing thoughts into mindful observations of my surroundings.

I release the need to fill every moment. I find peace in simplicity.

I limit digital distractions to truly experience each interaction and activity.

I let go of multitasking and give my full presence to each task.

I infuse care and creativity into small daily acts like cooking, cleaning, and getting ready.

I spend time in nature daily to gain perspective and restore my spirit.

I give compassionate attention to my thoughts, emotions, and body signals throughout the day.

I embrace moments of joy and lightness, letting laughter restore and rejuvenate me.

I celebrate small blessings and kindnesses from loved ones and strangers alike.

I search for beauty around me, using it as a portal back to the present.

I lean into moments of wonder and awe inspired by nature, art, people, and animals.

When busy thoughts creep back in, I gently return my focus to the here and now.

I replace harsh self-talk with patient understanding of my needs in this moment.

I release fixation on past regrets and future worries, redirecting my mind to this breath, this step, this task.

I let each moment unfold without trying to control or rush time. There is purpose in every present moment.

I forgive myself when my mind wanders, and simply redirect it with gentleness and love.

I embrace doing nothing at times. In stillness, I reconnect with my inner knowing and wisdom.

I remember that presence is a practice. Each moment I can begin again.

I honor the process of awakening to the beauty of each present moment.

With childlike wonder, I open myself to the gifts offered by each moment.

I let go of judgments and experience moments with fresh eyes and an open heart.

Presence grounds me in gratitude for all I have already been given.

I release the need for big experiences, finding peace in walks, meals, and loving connection.

Tuning into my senses connects me deeply with the world around me.

Simple rituals like tea, prayer, or journaling help center me in the moment.

I let my tedious tasks become moving meditations, keeping my mind immersed in the present activity.

I honor rest and relaxation as sacred acts, not luxuries I don't have time for.

I set healthy limits on devices and entertainment that steal my presence.

Time with loved ones is precious. I give them my full attention.

I let inspiration for future plans arise from a deep connection to the present.

Mindfulness unveils solutions I couldn't see when overwhelmed and scattered.

I embrace spontaneity and find joy in detours from my planned agenda.

As I open to the present, I gain clarity over what truly matters most to me.

I let nature's healing rhythms guide my movements - waking with the sun, bed by moonlight.

I forgive past versions of myself for not recognizing the beauty around me. Each moment offers renewal.

I embrace moments of creative expression through writing, crafting, playing, and moving my body.

As I open my heart, inspiration and creative solutions pour in.

I let the lightness of play infuse my tasks and interactions. Joy makes me present.

I detach from roles and identities to experience each moment with fresh authenticity.

I let my senses anchor me in the physical world while my spirit remains unbounded.

With deep breaths, I center myself in the safety and infinite potential of this moment.

MY NOTES

Self-care
IS EMPOWERMENT

Chapter Five

Harnessing Resilience In Overcoming Challenges

Life offers up endless challenges - big and small. Some we actively seek out, while others seem to appear unexpectedly, throwing our balance off. It's easy to get overwhelmed by the obstacles we must continually overcome as part of this human experience. But within each challenge lies an opportunity for growth.

This chapter provides affirmations to help you harness your inner resilience when faced with daily struggles and setbacks. Instead of being debilitated by hardship, you'll learn to move through challenges with adaptability, wisdom, and grace.

The coming affirmations will guide you in developing unshakeable faith in your ability to persist and heal. You'll be reminded of previous obstacles you worked through, unearthing strength you can call on now. Rather than play the victim when challenged, you can evolve into the victorious heroine of your story.

You have been gifted with profound resilience and untapped courage. You have overcome before and will again now. When you face each day's struggles with fortitude, you inspire hope in others too. Together we realize that with willing hearts, no challenge can keep us down for long. Rise up strong one, with head held high.

Affirmations

I meet each challenge with resilience, wisdom, and unwavering faith in my ability to overcome.

I harness the lessons from past obstacles, knowing they've given me tools and strength.

I do not let setbacks define or discourage me. They are stepping stones on my journey.

I stand tall in the face of hardship, embracing my unshakeable spirit.

I adapt to whatever comes my way. Flexibility and flow are my superpowers.

I release the need for control. With willingness, I work with life's twists and turns.

I forgive myself for moments when my strength wavered. Now I know better.

I remain openhanded when plans unravel. New possibilities arise.

I embrace uncertainty as part of life's adventure. With courage, I step forward.

I trust in my inner guidance to navigate me through stormy seas.

I let go of fear-based thinking. I use challenges to unlock my highest potential.

I tune out discouraging voices, trusting my own inner wisdom.

What once felt hard is now easy. I build my resilience muscle each day.

I flow with the seasons, harnessing their energies to work through life's trials.

I stand in my power when others try to invalidate my truth. Peacefully, I hold my ground.

Constructive criticism helps me grow. Destructive judgment I let wash over me. I know my own heart.

I embrace challenges as teachers, showing me what I must cultivate within.

With deep care for myself and others, I set needed boundaries.

I let go of relationships, stories and roles that no longer feed my spirit. Forward motion matters most.

I soften my grip on the familiar, opening myself to new lessons and blessings.

I bear hardship with grace, letting it strengthen, not harden my heart.

I meet anger with patience and unkindness with compassion.

Though my mind forgets, my spirit always remembers the light within me and within others. That light is our unbreakable bond.

When I lose my way, I pause and reconnect with my inner compass and the wisdom of my heart.

I have faith that each challenge occurs for a reason, even if I cannot yet see it. I trust in life's unfolding.

I welcome support while knowing that my strength comes from within.

I am the hero, not the victim, of my story. Every struggle reveals more of my courage and brilliance.

Difficult times call me inward to harness my inner fortitude and remember what matters most.

After hardship, I emerge wiser and more powerful than before. Like gold in a furnace, I am refined.

I honor the grief and growth that come hand in hand. One cannot exist without the other.

Challenges test my character but never diminish my worth. I always deserve love.

With patience and compassion, I unpack my learnings and integrate wisdom from every experience.

The challenges I walk through now will serve me later. This too shall pass.

I soften around life's sharp edges. With grace, I adapt and endure.

I embrace the bittersweet gifts of impermanence - change, loss and renewal go hand in hand.

I remember laughter, joy, and lightness will always return, even when momentarily eclipsed by clouds. Stay hopeful.

When I feel depleted, I know wellsprings of strength still run deep within me, waiting to be unearthed.

I channel anger and frustration's powerful, creative energy into courageous action.

Hard times call me to embody gentleness, patience, and love more fully - they are needed most in darkness. I rise to answer.

I let passion, not fear or scarcity, motivate me through difficult times.

I welcome guidance and validation but do not make them prerequisites for self-belief. My inner compass guides me on.

I may bend but will not break. Within me lies resilience beyond measure.

I flow with the inevitability of change. Expecting life's fluctuations brings me calm and courage amidst them.

Each new dawn offers renewal. Yesterday's scars need not define today's path.

Whatever lies ahead, I know I have survived 100% of my worst days thus far. I've got this.

MY NOTES

Self-care
IS EMPOWERMENT

Chapter Six

Nurturing Relationships And Setting Boundaries

Our relationships profoundly shape our lives and sense of self. But society often teaches us that being "nice" means being a doormat - endlessly sacrificing our needs to please others. In the process, we can lose touch with our own boundaries and desires.

This chapter offers affirmations to help you nurture relationships rooted in mutual love, respect, and understanding. You'll be guided to set compassionate boundaries that honor both your needs and those of others.

The coming affirmations will remind you that your wants and values matter. You'll learn to speak up unapologetically for yourself while also being a generous, actively engaged partner.

Healthy connections require self-care and honesty. Your light dims when you give too much of yourself away. Shine bright by offering your spirit, never compromising it. Are you ready to celebrate meaningful bonds that help both you and your loved ones thrive? The most fulfilling relationships unveil your highest self.

Affirmations

I lovingly care for myself so I may fully show up in my relationships.

I embrace open communication and dedicate time to nourish my relationships.

I give relationship difficulties patience, knowing storms only make us stronger.

I release relationships that dim my light. I seek bonds that help me shine brighter.

I welcome support while taking responsibility for my own growth and healing.

I honor others' journeys without losing focus on my own path.

I speak my needs and truths with clarity, care, and confidence.

I know setting boundaries means I value myself and others.

I forgive past versions of myself for not asking for what I needed. I know better now.

I let go of resentment and gently communicate my boundaries.

I give myself time and space to regroup when I feel depleted.

I embrace alone time to reconnect with myself before rejoining others.

I accept support and sustain myself through challenging times.

I nurture my body, mind, and spirit daily so I may give from a full vessel.

I release relationships based solely on past comfort or convenience. My connections reflect who I am now.

I welcome growth, change, and imperfection in relationships. With compassion, we evolve together.

I offer support freely but not so much that I exhaust myself. Balance benefits us both.

I embrace that my needs and paths may diverge from loved ones. We wish each other well.

I let go of past hurts with forgiveness. Our shared humanity matters most.

I acknowledge different perspectives with empathy while standing firm in my truth.

I give myself time to process and heal emotional injuries before reacting. Patience brings peace.

I remain openhearted even when trust is tested. Wisdom grows through adversity.

I tune out voices of manipulation or cruelty. I listen to those who speak with care.

I release guilt over outgrowing situations that once nourished me. I honor my expansion.

I embrace mutual growth, not fixing or changing others. We each walk our own path.

I welcome support from loved ones who celebrate the real me.

I let go of superficial bonds, making space for relationships of meaning, understanding, and mutual growth.

I express my needs; I cannot expect loved ones to intuit what I do not voice.

I welcome constructive feedback from trusted sources. Blind loyalty does not serve my growth.

I take time to emotionally reconnect before discussing issues. A strong foundation supports hard talks.

I speak my truth while also validating others' perspectives. Our differences need not divide us.

I release the need for constant contact or reassurance from others. I trust our bond's strength.

I embrace the natural ebb and flow of relationships. Harmony lies in the space between notes.

I let kindness, empathy, and forgiveness guide me in resolving conflict.

I honor others' boundaries and needs as I honor my own. Balance sustains us.

I step back to reflect before reacting. Wisdom aligns my words with care, truth, and facts.

I welcome my loved ones' support. Their encouragement fuels my growth.

I let go of how things "should" be. With compassion, I accept each relationship's natural evolution.

I embrace that letting go of some relationships makes space for meaningful new connections.

I give myself time to process, reflect, and heal before committing deeply again.

I tune into my intuition and inner knowing to guide me to kindred spirits and communities.

I take action to nurture my most life-giving relationships and disconnect from those causing me harm.

I forgive past betrayals, so my spirit stays open to receive new blessings.

I embrace life's changing seasons, knowing joy, sorrow, union, and loss all play their part.

I honor others' journeys while never losing sight of my own path and purpose.

With wisdom and care, I water the seeds of relationships that help us both grow into our highest selves.

MY NOTES

Self-care
IS EMPOWERMENT

Chapter Seven

Thriving In Career And Personal Ambitions

Modern life often equates our worth with productivity and professional success. In the hustle to climb ladders and impress others, we can lose connection with the types of work and achievements that truly feed our spirit.

This chapter offers empowering affirmations to help you thrive in your career and personal ambitions without burning out. You'll be guided to release unhealthy pressures and find joy in meaningful work that suits your skills and values.

The coming affirmations will help you celebrate small wins while maintaining perspective on what matters most - your health, purpose, and connections. You'll be reminded that you are worthy beyond any worldly definitions of "success."

The goal of this path is to get to a place where you can take pride in your job because it reflects who you truly are. Titles and trophies play only a small role. What counts most is fulfilling your potential through uplifting action each day. Are you ready to feel proud of your growth and achievements without making them the sole markers of your worth? Take heart, your purpose starts with being, not doing.

Affirmations

I embrace work that energizes me and utilizes my gifts to make a difference.

I celebrate my skills while remaining open to learning and growth.

I work with purpose, letting my heart guide me, not outside expectations.

I release the need to constantly prove my worth through achievement. I am enough.

My value stems from my spirit, not my productivity or job title.

I welcome abundance without making it the sole marker of my success.

I tune out criticism, trusting my inner wisdom to guide my actions.

Each day, I appreciate small accomplishments that move me toward my dreams.

I embrace work-life balance, honoring both my professional and personal needs.

I give myself permission to rest and reset when overwhelmed. My health comes first.

I let passion, not pressure, drive my work. Enthusiasm energizes me.

I detach from difficult coworkers and challenges by remembering my purpose.

I stay focused on the next right step. Each one leads me forward.

Constructive feedback helps me grow. Destructive criticism I let wash over me.

I embrace uncertainty in my professional life, flowing with each new opportunity.

With courage, I envision the boldest expression of my purpose and take steps to pursue it.

I welcome collaboration while also taking quiet time to connect with my vision.

I release the need for everything to be perfect. Progress empowers me.

I tune out jealous voices, knowing there is abundance for all.

I let go of competition, comparing myself only to my past self.

Each day, I appreciate those who lifted me up and paved the way for my achievements.

The pace of nature balances my urge to hustle. All things in due time.

I exercise patience with the process, knowing reaching my goals requires small steps.

I acknowledge my brilliance and talents. The world needs what I have to offer.

I detach my self-worth from any one employer, title or project. I am the constant.

I celebrate both planned accomplishments and spontaneous opportunities. Joyful flexibility keeps me thriving.

I welcome support on the journey without needing others' validation. My worth is innate.

I let go of roles, titles and work that no longer light me up. Make space for what sparks joy.

I value progress and learning over perfection. Each experience expands my gifts.

I embrace work-life integration, finding opportunities to express my purpose across all areas of life.

I give myself permission to step back, recalibrate, and ensure my ambitions align with my truth.

I acknowledge when things feel off-track and gracefully correct my course. My inner compass guides me.

I release attachment to specific outcomes. Fulfillment stems from my commitment and process.

Criticism may sting but never defines me. I know myself and my own heart.

I let go of the familiar to make space for work that taps my full potential.

I embrace that my path unfolds day by day. Each moment reflects where I am now.

With compassion, I observe old fears and patterns playing out. Then I consciously move forward.

I infuse playfulness into my work to stay energized, engaged, and creative.

I celebrate teamwork and guiding others while also honoring independent time to create.

I welcome support and validation from loved ones who champion my professional journey.

I detach my identity and ego from any one employer or title. Those are roles, not my essence.

I acknowledge when I need rest and renewal. Burnout stifles my spirit. Self-care kindles it.

Things ebb and flow in cycles. Challenging times today plant seeds for future bounty.

My worth remains unchanged by any accomplishments or setbacks. Growth, not greatness, fulfills me.

I embrace work as an act of service, contributing my gifts to make a positive difference.

───── ✻ ─────

Each day, I appreciate the chance to express purpose through my path, impacting my small corner.

# MY NOTES

Self-care
IS EMPOWERMENT

Chapter Eight

Prioritizing Self In Daily Life

It's so easy to get caught up caring for others that we neglect our own basic needs. We rush through days fueled by coffee, drained by demands, all while our inner light dims from lack of nourishment. But self-care is not selfish - it's an act of self-love that allows us to contribute meaningfully.

This chapter provides affirmations to help you honor your needs unapologetically amidst life's duties. You'll be reminded of the power of regular self-care practices that refresh your mind, body, and spirit.

The coming affirmations will guide you in taking time for activities that spark joy, calm your nervous system, and remind you of your inherent worth. You'll learn to tune out the guilt and stop viewing self-care as a luxury only permitted once other obligations are met.

Make yourself a priority each day, not just when you have permission. Your light shines brightest when your whole being is nurtured. Are you ready to celebrate prioritizing your self-love and self-care? You deserve it now - just as you are.

Affirmations

I lovingly care for and nourish myself daily. My needs matter.

I honor my energy limits and take breaks to refuel myself.

I give myself permission to rest and relax without guilt. It sustains me.

I embrace self-care practices that spark my joy and wellbeing.

I detach my worth from productivity. I deserve rest.

I tune out critical inner voices and nurture myself with compassion.

I set boundaries around my time and energy. My health depends on it.

I celebrate acts of self-love, no matter how small. I am worthy.

I make space each day for activities that center and calm me.

I honor my needs without apology or explanation. I matter.

I release guilt over outgrowing situations that no longer nourish me.

I give myself time to recharge between giving energy to others.

I embrace saying no without guilt. My priorities matter.

I detach from draining relationships and activities to conserve my energy.

I nourish my mind, body, and spirit daily. Balance fills me up.

I let go of perfectionism and make peace with progress.

I allow myself to rest and do nothing at times. My worth is unchanged.

I trust my inner wisdom to know what I need in each moment.

I welcome support when overwhelmed. I don't have to do it all alone.

I forgive myself when I neglect my own needs. Every moment offers renewal.

I own my priorities unapologetically. My life reflects my values.

I embrace saying no without justifying it. No is a complete sentence.

I detach my self-worth from others' demands on my time and energy.

I celebrate small acts of self-care that honor the sanctuary of my spirit.

I let go of satisfying others at the expense of myself. My needs matter too.

I allow myself to access feel-good activities, foods, and experiences that light me up.

I set aside time each day just for myself to recharge at my own pace.

I lean into supportive communities and relationships where I feel replenished.

I embrace rest as productive when it fuels my clarity and creativity.

I detach my self-worth from duty, productivity, and accomplishing daily checklists.

I let go of multitasking and give my full presence to each activity.

I honor my ever-changing needs. Some seasons call for gentle self-care, others for bold self-expression. I listen within.

I soften my grip on plans and schedules to enjoy unstructured time.

I embrace spending time alone to reconnect with my intuition and inner wisdom, apart from others' demands.

I nurture my nervous system and sensitive side. My vulnerability is a gift, not a weakness.

I let the pace and rhythms of nature guide my self-care practices.

I release expectations that I should always put others' needs before my own. Prioritizing myself allows me to help others from a place of surplus, not scarcity.

I unwrap life's small pleasures and enjoy indulgences that reconnect me to my senses.

I embrace my need for creative expression through arts, music, writing, or hobbies. Making time to create lights me up from within.

I celebrate acts of nourishment, comfort, and care for this one precious body and mind that let me experience life.

I tune in to my unique symptoms of stress and meet them with gentleness. I listen rather than push through.

I honor seasons when my spirit calls me inward for restoration away from crowds and stimulation. Solitude recharges me.

I appreciate all this vessel does for me. With loving care, I nourish it as the temple of my spirit.

I celebrate myself fully - who I am, who I am becoming, and who I wish to be. I embrace all that I am.

MY NOTES

Self-care
IS EMPOWERMENT

Chapter Nine

Discovering Purpose And Inner Peace

Nowadays, we can easily lose touch with our deeper purpose and inner peace. Endless distractions keep our attention scattered on the surface of things. We forget to go within and nourish our spiritual selves.

This chapter offers empowering affirmations to guide you in reconnecting with your unique purpose and innate tranquility. The affirmations will remind you to regularly go inward to rediscover what most matters to your spirit.

You'll be encouraged to celebrate moments of stillness, clarity, and alignment with your truth. As superficial stresses and demands on your time fade into the background, you'll gain perspective on your authentic purpose and priorities.

You already contain vast wisdom within that unveils your reason for being. Your inner light guides you to meaning, joy, and serenity. Are you ready to discover your highest self and make peace with where you are right now? Your purpose starts with embracing the present.

Affirmations

I make time each day to connect with my inner wisdom, apart from the world's distractions.

I embrace moments of solitude to gain clarity on my purpose and priorities.

I release the need to know exactly where I'm headed. My purpose unfolds step-by-step.

I let go of chasing superficial signs of success. My worth is innate, not earned.

I tune out my busy mind and tune into my peaceful inner sanctuary.

I trust my inner guidance to lead me to people and places that nourish my spirit.

I welcome opportunities to help others while keeping balance with self-care.

I embrace stillness and spend time in nature to gain perspective.

I let go of preconceived notions of what my purpose "should" look like. I stay open.

I forgive the past and honor this moment as a clean slate to live my purpose.

My purpose starts with my presence - being fully in the now, where life happens.

I release the need for big, bold action and trust subtle intuition.

I welcome inspiration and synchronicity as signs I'm on the right path.

I embrace imperfection - my purpose does not demand perfectionism.

I celebrate small steps on the path, knowing they lead me to my highest self.

I let go of stories that shrink my purpose. My gifts are needed in this world.

I release the need to justify my desires. My soul's longing leads me forward.

I make time for creativity and self-expression - gifts to access purpose.

I know life unfolds day by day. By living my truth now, my purpose is unveiled.

I welcome peace and joy into my life, allowing them to guide my actions.

I let my heart's wisdom, not others' expectations, shape my purpose.

I embrace where I am now while envisioning where I wish to be. Patience and faith empower me.

I celebrate moments of awe and inspiration that reconnect me to my purpose.

I trust uncertainty. Relinquishing control reveals my purpose in due time.

I release the need for constant motion and stimulation. Peace often reveals itself in stillness.

I make time for inner inquiry through meditation, journaling, and reflection. Self-discovery requires tuning out distractions.

I welcome support and guidance that aligns with my truth. My inner voice remains the ultimate guide.

I appreciate each day's opportunities and blessings, though seemingly small. My purpose is unveiled moment by moment.

I embrace my changing purpose as I grow. Each phase prepares me for the next.

I let go of self-criticism. With compassion, I acknowledge my greatness.

I celebrate times of joy, laughter, and creativity. Levity sustains me.

I release the need for immediate results. Personal growth cannot be rushed. I focus on the process.

I trust life's unseen forces are guiding me where I need to be. Synchronicity is confirmation I'm on the right path.

I make time for wonder and play, like my child self. These unveil my purpose.

I practice being over doing. Simply embracing each moment is purposeful.

My search for meaning begins within. External pursuits alone will not fulfill me.

I welcome my continuously evolving purpose. Growth comes through change.

I appreciate all who walked this path before me. I follow the footsteps of those who live their truth.

I release the need for big revelations. Simplicity and subtlety often hold profound purpose.

I make peace with uncertainty. The unknown contains gifts I can't yet see.

I embrace my changing priorities and interests, knowing they reflect my growth. My purpose is not static.

I welcome action that makes a difference in myself and others. Start small.

I celebrate my "why" - the passion and meaning behind my actions. This drives me more than outcomes.

Each day, I rediscover my light within. My purpose starts with embracing the wholeness already inside me.

MY NOTES

Self-care
IS EMPOWERMENT

Conclusion

We've reached the end of our year-long journey of unveiling your highest potential through daily affirmations. I hope you've found as much inspiration, wisdom, and empowerment in these words as I have.

Looking back, I trust you are not the same person you were when we began. While the transformation has occurred incrementally, these subtle shifts in self-perception and belief accumulate into profound positive change over time.

Trust that believing in your worth, strength, and abilities wasn't just an act of blind faith. The magnificence we uncovered was there within you all along, patiently waiting to be brought into your awareness.

My hope is that through regular affirmation practice, you've dismantled old patterns of self-criticism and limiting beliefs. While our inner critics may still occasionally whisper doubts, remember you now have the tools to recognize and release that self-diminishing narrative.

I encourage you to continue your affirmation practice as you feel called, adapting it to your evolving needs. Jot down your favorite affirmations in a journal so you can continue reflecting on these empowering messages.

This book merely sparked the unveiling process - the real transformation unfolds through your ongoing commitment to self-love and inner growth. Know that you have cultivated the wisdom and resilience to navigate all that lies ahead.

Remember, the incredible force within you is just waiting to be expressed each day through your words, actions, and essence. Stay committed to your luminosity. The world needs your light.

With faith in your inner strength, continue stepping boldly in the direction of your dreams, purpose, and highest self. Your magnificent spirit deserves to be celebrated. May you embrace your radiance in each moment. You've got this!

Bonus – Nine Transformative Routines for Women

As we conclude our exploration of empowering affirmations, I want to focus on how we can turn inspiration into action through daily self-care routines. Real change requires implementing small practices consistently over time.

Let's reflect on what self-care means to each of us individually. Consider these questions:

- What specific activities help you feel replenished in body, mind and spirit?
- How do you know when you need to pause and care for yourself?
- Are there certain routines that provide a sense of

grounding and calm?

Aim for a balance between indulgence and nourishing self-care. True self-care restores and revitalizes us, enabling us to show up as our best selves in all areas of life. Routines that deplete or distract us don't cultivate lasting wellbeing.

Establishing even small consistent practices makes self-care attainable amidst busy lives. The key is to intentionally integrate self-care into each day. Micro-practices throughout your routine quickly compound into transformation.

With mindful daily routines focused on mental, emotional, physical and spiritual health, you honor your whole self continuously. Are you ready to make self-care a non-negotiable practice? Let's explore some rejuvenating routines to begin caring for your whole being.

Reflect on Your Self-Care Practice

Take 15-30 minutes to intentionally reflect on how you currently care for yourself across body, mind and spirit. Consider these prompts:

- What specific activities make you feel happy, peaceful, recharged, or creative? Make a list of things that light you up or help release stress.

- How do you know when you need to pause and give yourself rest or nourishment? Do you wait until you're utterly exhausted? Learn your unique signals it's time for self-care.

- How often do you take breaks in your day or week just

for you? Is there room to build in more rejuvenating mini-practices?

- Which simple self-care rituals provide a sense of grounding, calm, or comfort? Can you expand or enhance these?

- Is your self-care balanced between indulgence and activities that energize you? Or mostly fleeting guilty pleasures? Reflect on how to cultivate sustaining practices.

- Are you compassionate with yourself if you miss self-care time? Or harshly critical? Cultivate self-forgiveness and flexibility.

Regularly checking in through reflection ensures your self-care adapts as your needs change. Make time to intentionally re-evaluate your rituals so they align with your evolving self. Consistent self-care sustains you through all of life's changes and challenges.

Disconnect and Have a Screenless Day

It's all too easy to let screens and devices consume our attention from morning to night. Taking regular screen breaks can profoundly improve physical and mental health.

Designate one day a week to go completely screen-free. Turn off phones, tablets, computers, TVs, and any other devices with displays. Use this as an opportunity to:

- Tune into your thoughts, feelings, and physical sensations without distraction. When's the last time you checked in with yourself?

- Engage your natural creativity through art, writing, music, dance, or hands-on projects. Enjoy self-expression beyond social media.

- Spend time outdoors connecting with nature. Go for walks, read under a tree, or have a picnic at the park.

- Be fully present with loved ones without interrupting conversations to check notifications.

- Try new hobbies or activities like gardening, hiking, learning an instrument, photography, or crafts.

- Cook, clean, and care for your space mindfully without background TV or scrolling through your phone.

- Do self-care activities like luxurious baths, self-massage, meditation, or sipping tea.

When you unplug regularly, you'll gain perspective on your device use and consciously choose your screen time. A tech detox clears mental clutter so you can access inner wisdom. Rejuvenate through the power of being fully offline.

Read a Book

Set aside time to curl up with a good book that transports and inspires you. Reading has numerous benefits for your mind and emotional health. It reduces stress, improves focus and memory, and enhances empathy, imagination and communication skills.

Make reading a soothing act of self-care. Choose books that either deepen your knowledge on meaningful topics or provide a blissful temporary escape from daily life. Select stories that connect with your spirit - perhaps memoirs of admirable figures, nature writing filled with beautiful imagery, poetry that stirs your soul, or fantasy novels that sweep you away to magical worlds.

Let reading transport your mind and restore your energy. Turn off devices, get cozy with a warm drink, find a serene spot, and indulge your literary wanderlust. Immerse yourself fully in the book you've chosen. Let the words soak into your spirit. Reading fulfilling books is a wonderful ritual of self-love.

Eat a Simple Healthy Meal

Preparing a nourishing meal just for yourself is a wonderful act of self-care that benefits body and spirit. Take time to mindfully plan, purchase, and cook a simple healthy meal or snack. Consider trying:

- A new recipe with seasonal ingredients from the farmer's market or your garden

- A comfort food from childhood made in a more nutritious way

- Exploring the cuisine from a culture you're unfamiliar with

- Hand-preparing fresh juices, smoothies, or tea blends with healing ingredients

- Making a shared meal for family or friends using beloved recipes

- Double batches of healthy meals and freeze for quick access when busy

- Packing homemade lunches or snacks to carry love with you throughout your day

Eating whole foods you've prepared with care fills you physically and emotionally in a way fast food can't. Dedicate time to planning, shopping with awareness, and savoring the cooking ritual itself. Infuse the food with love for yourself and others.

Simple nourishing meals ground you in self-care while also benefiting your health, energy levels, and even mood. Make eating in a sacred act of honoring your body's needs.

Practice a Hobby

Making time for hobbies you feel passionate about is an important act of self-care. When you tap into activities that enliven your spirit and spark joy, it provides a sense of deep nourishment.

Reflect on pastimes that put you into a state of flow and bring out your creativity. Consider exploring new hobbies or immerse yourself in lifelong ones that you've neglected. Choose activities that feel energizing and make you lose track of time.

Hobbies that reconnect you with your passions unlock reserves of energy and inspiration. They allow you to immerse all your senses and express your unique gifts, often in ways your daily routine doesn't allow.

Fully absorb yourself in your chosen hobby. Let yourself get swept up in the smells, textures, sights, and sounds. Follow where inspiration leads you. Approach the hobby with child-like wonder and delight.

When you make time for playfulness, creativity, and joy, you'll discover new aspects of yourself. Hobbies that ignite your spirit become powerful rituals of self-care. They reveal your inner light waiting to shine.

See a Friend

Meaningful human connection is vital for wellbeing. Isolation can quickly lead to stagnation, loneliness, and depressive thoughts. Make seeing friends a consistent self-care ritual.

Reach out to a trusted friend or two you feel most yourself around. Schedule video chats, phone calls, meet-ups for coffee/meals, or activity dates like:

- Museum, gallery, boutique browsing
- Hiking, yoga, workout classes
- Crafting, baking, gardening together
- Attending concerts, festivals, markets
- Game nights, movie marathons
- Cooking and enjoying meals together

- Volunteering for a cause you care about

Even quick check-ins make a difference. Share funny stories, vent about challenges, ask for advice, or offer support. Feel energized by laughter, nostalgia, and promising dreams.

Devote quality time to just being present together, without distractions. Cherish friends who know and nurture your real self. Make nurturing your social connections a priority. You'll both feel more rooted in purpose.

Give Yourself a Hug

Human touch is profoundly healing, even if it's just your own embrace. Taking a moment to consciously wrap your arms around yourself in a hug releases oxytocin, provides comfort, and reminds you of your inherent worthiness of love.

Choose times during your day to mindfully practice self-hugging. Perhaps during stressful moments, before bed for comfort, or anytime you need reassurance.

Start with hands gently resting on your shoulders. Slowly wrap your arms around front and fully encircle your torso. Gently stroke your back or cup the back of your head. Sway slowly side to side if that adds comfort.

Breathe deeply and soak in the sensation of being cradled in your own loving hold. Release any tension in your body. Know that you are safe and supported.

Make self-hugging a consistent practice. Turn it into muscle memory you can access anytime, anywhere for quick calming reassurance. This simple ritual comforts your inner child, builds self-esteem, and helps you feel grounded and secure within.

Spend Time in Nature

Being out in nature profoundly restores mental, emotional, and physical wellbeing. Getting outside into fresh air and surrounded by the sights and sounds of the natural world nourishes us on many levels.

Make spending regular time outdoors part of your self-care routine. Consider:

- Local parks, hiking trails, lakes, rivers, beaches
- Your own backyard, patio or balcony
- Community gardens, nature preserves, botanical gardens
- Camping trips, cabins in the woods, glamping adventures

Tune into the sensory pleasures - bird song, rustling leaves, fragrant flowers, the feeling of grass under bare feet. Let your senses come alive.

Practice forest bathing by strolling aimlessly, sitting against a tree, lying on the earth. Absorb the healing energies.

Try grounding techniques like walking barefoot on soil. Synchronize your breath with the tides. Feel your connection to the planet.

However you choose to immerse yourself, make regular nature time a priority. Our innate bond with nature restores our spirits like nothing else can.

Do Something Creative

Engaging in creative, expressive activities provides a fulfilling outlet for stress while also boosting your mood. When you're feeling depleted, make time to let your creativity flow freely.

Activities like painting, drawing, pottery, and DIY crafts allow you to work with your hands and tangibly produce something beautiful. Or play music, sing, dance, or write stories, plays or poetry to tap into your inner artist.

For inspiration, delve into Pinterest or YouTube tutorials on everything from watercolor techniques to mini clay figurines. Gather supplies from craft stores, thrift shops, or even household items.

Don't judge the outcome. Release perfectionism and just enjoy the creative process. Savor the sensations of your chosen medium. Become one with the music. Let your imagination wander and spill out untamed.

Immerse yourself fully in free-flowing creativity whenever you need an energy boost or emotional release. Let inspiration lead the way and uncover hidden passions. Nurture your inner artist.

Dear reader,

Thank you for joining me and engaging wholeheartedly with these empowering affirmations.

I sincerely hope this book provided motivation, inspiration, and a constant reminder of your inner strengths. If these affirmations made a positive impact on your life, **I kindly ask you to consider leaving a review on Amazon sharing your thoughts**. Your reviews mean so much, and help other women who are seeking empowerment find this book. Leaving your perspective is quick, easy, and such a gift to both me and other readers.

I wish you endless affirmative days ahead!

With gratitude,

Emma Bennett

EXCLUSIVE BONUS: YOUR AUDIOBOOK AWAITS!

Dear valued reader,
We understand that life gets busy, and sometimes, you might not have the time to sit down with a book. As an exclusive bonus, we've created an audiobook version just for you! Now you can enjoy daily affirmations on-the-go, anytime, anywhere.

Simply scan the QR code below to start your audio journey of empowerment.

ALSO BY EMMA BENNETT

"I Choose Me - Self-Care Workbook for Empowered Women"

If you've been inspired by "I Am Worthy," take the next step in your self-care journey with "I Choose Me." This workbook is a comprehensive guide designed to help you prioritize yourself in a world that often demands too much.

"I Choose Me" offers practical exercises, insightful questions, and empowering activities to help you discover your true self. It's not just a book; it's a transformative experience that will help you establish healthy boundaries, cultivate self-love, and live a life filled with purpose.

Available now on Amazon.